THE WORLD HERITAGE

THE EMPIRE OF THE CZARS

CHILDRENS PRESS®
CHICAGO

Table of Contents

Library of Congress Cataloging-in-Publication Data

Carrion, Esther.
   [Imperio de los Zares. English]
   The Empire of the Czars / by Esther Carrion.
     p.   cm. — (The World heritage)
   Includes index.
   ISBN 0-516-08319-0
   1. Russia—Description and travel—Juvenile literature. 2. Russia—History—
Juvenile literature. [1. Russia.] I. Title. II. Series.
DK29.C37513 1994
947—dc20
                                        94-16114
                                         CIP
                                         AC

El imperio de los Zares: © INCAFO S.A./Ediciones S.M./UNESCO 1992
The Empire of the Czars: © Childrens Press, Inc./UNESCO 1994

ISBN (UNESCO) 92-3-102698-4
ISBN (Childrens Press) 0-516-08319-0

The Empire of the Czars

Russia is a vast and mysterious land, sprawling across both Europe and Asia. Its ethnic diversity, the little-known customs of its people, and its isolation from the rest of Europe in past centuries add to the sense that it is a land apart.

Geographically, Russia is gigantic. There are rivers that run for thousands of miles, lakes as big as oceans, beautiful evergreen forests, barren steppes that have defeated invincible armies, and the immense, desolate Siberian plain. Travel was never easy in this enormous territory, which had little access to the navigable sea.

All this and more was the Russia of the czars. ("Czar," or "tsar" in Russian, means "emperor." It comes from the Latin word "Caesar.")

Countless ethnic groups inhabited Russia, and many continue to live there today. Among them were the Slavs of the south, from the lands along the Dnieper River; and the northerly Rus who, after centuries of obscurity, built the Russian state. Out of this diversity emerged a national spirit. Constant expansion and conquest led to the formation of the Czarist Empire of the seventeenth and eighteenth centuries.

But despite centuries of unity under the empire, Russia remains a diverse society, with a multitude of languages, religions, and ways of life. To speak of just one Russia is to overlook the geographic, historical, and social realities of this immense land.

The New Russia
With its wealth of Baroque and Neo-Classical buildings, the beautiful city of St. Petersburg symbolizes Peter the Great's dream of a new Russia. Most of the early buildings are the work of the Italian architects Domenico Tressini and Bartolomeo Rastrelli. The Smolny Convent, whose main facade is shown in this photo, was built following Rastrelli's design.

The Beginnings

The earliest known people in Russia lived on the southern steppe near the Black Sea. They were nomadic tribes, among them Scythians and Persians.

On the shores of the Black Sea, these people came into contact with Greek colonists in the seventh and eighth centuries B.C. They soon began to trade goods with the Greeks and to be influenced by their culture.

This relationship with the Greeks lasted until the territory fell under the influence of the Roman Empire, and later the Byzantine Empire and the Abbasid Caliphate. Eventually, the Slavs settled in the region.

The Slavic peoples of the south, influenced by these ancient empires, established towns along the fertile banks of the Dnieper and Dniester Rivers. Trade was their chief occupation.

Meanwhile, what was happening on the central steppe and in the northern forests?

We know much less about the remote history of these regions. However, we do know that they were inhabited by Finnic, Baltic, and Slavic nomads. Their way of life was far more primitive than that of the people to the south. They lived in small, independent groups under local chiefs. The chiefs marked out their territories along the Volga and the Western Dvina rivers south of Lakes Ladoga and Onega.

The Fortress on the Hill
The fortress of the Kremlin, whose design is seen at the lower left, is a walled enclosure covering 70 acres (28 hectares). It is triangular in form. Outside the walls lies the immense Red Square. In the upper right photo we see one of the buildings that faces the square: the City Historical Museum. In the lower photo are some of the twenty-nine towers that guard the walls.

1. Cathedral of the Annunciation
2. Cathedral of the Archangel Michael
3. Cathedral of the Dormition
4. The Hall of Facets
5. St. Catherine's Church
6. Cathedral of the Savior
7. Church of the Virgin's Nativity
8. Church of the Twelve Apostles

These two distant worlds—the people of the north and the people of the south—finally met early in the sixth century. Slavic groups began to expand across the Russian plain. Spreading northward, they conquered the nomadic tribes. In the south, they expanded along the great rivers, founding such cities as Kiev in the sixth to seventh centuries and Rostov in the ninth century.

Timeline

c. 6th–7th century A.D.	The city of Kiev is founded.
9th century	The city of Rostov is founded.
c. 980–1015	Vladimir the Great consolidates the State of Kiev. The Russian people are converted to Christianity.
c. 1050	Kiev's Cathedral of St. Sophia is completed.
1223	Genghis Khan's Mongol army defeats the army of Kiev, but withdraws.
1240	Kiev is attacked and plundered by the Mongols, who then establish control.
Early 1200s	The Principality of Moscow is established.
Late 1300s	The reconstruction of the Kremlin of Moscow gets underway.
1547	Ivan IV, "The Terrible," has himself crowned Czar (Emperor) of All the Russias.
1696	The effective reign of Peter the Great begins.
1703	Peter I founds St. Petersburg.
1762	Catherine II begins her reign.
1861	Czar Alexander II signs a decree abolishing serfdom.
1891	Work begins on the Trans-Siberian Railroad. Intensive colonization of Siberia.
1905	Bloody Sunday. Workers march on the Winter Palace of St. Petersburg; many are killed.
1917	The Socialist Revolution and the Bolshevik Revolution in Russia. End of the Russian Empire.
1922	The Union of Soviet Socialist Republics (USSR) is created.
1991	Disintegration of the USSR. Independence of the soviet republics. Birth of the Commonwealth of Independent States (CIS).

City with a European Court
St. Petersburg is the crowning achievement of Peter I, "The Great," who brought about the Europeanization of the empire. To fulfill his dream of a European-style empire, he rejected centuries-old Russian traditions and customs. In the upper photo is Palace Square. The lower photo shows a monument to Catherine II, who continued the work of Peter the Great, and the Fortress of Peter and Paul, designed by Tressini.

But this fragile Slavic unity did not last long. In the eighth century, the Slavs in the north were conquered by the Varangians, a warlike Scandinavian people who called themselves the "Rus." They soon controlled the region's economy, as well as the transportation routes along the Volga and the Dnieper. They formed the Principality of Kiev, the beginning of the Russian state.

The State of Kiev

The territory of the State of Kiev stretched from the great northern lakes to the Black Sea, and from the Baltic countries in the west to the eastern edge of Europe. The northern conquerors mingled with the more numerous Slavic peoples and soon absorbed much of the Slavic culture.

The city of Kiev was an all-important stop on the trade route to Constantinople (now Istanbul, Turkey). It became the political and administrative center of the state. In the tenth century the rulers and the Russian people turned to Christianity. They were converted by the Byzantine Church, centered in Constantinople. At that point, Kiev also became the religious center of "all the Russias." In the north was another important city, Novgorod, the hub for trade from the Arctic zone southward and westward.

With the reign of Vladimir I, "the Great" (known as St. Vladimir), at the beginning of the eleventh century, the State of Kiev entered a period of splendor. Trade was intense, the arts flourished, and contact with the outside world increased dramatically. Written chronicles of the time began to speak of "the land of Rus." The princes of Kiev heightened this national spirit and maintained it by forming a Royal Guard of nobles.

Nevertheless, it was impossible to keep the state from breaking apart. In the thirteenth century, the Mongols threatened the State of Kiev. In 1223 the army of the dreaded Genghis Khan defeated a Kievan army, and in 1240 Kiev itself was attacked. A wave of terror, plunder, and desolation swept across the steppe and through the northern forests. First the Mongols, and later their successors the Golden Horde, ruled the steppe and made the Russian princes their vassals.

In the midst of this upheaval and desolation, a new Russian state formed in the north: the Principality of Moscow.

The Difficult Task of Reconstruction
Over the years, the city of Kiev has endured many hardships that have affected its preservation. Nonetheless, thanks to reconstruction, we can admire today these buildings of great historic and artistic value. The top photo is a view of the city, and below is the Kiev Opera.

From the Principality of Moscow to Czarist Russia

The Principality of Moscow—or Muscovy, as it was called at that time—was formed during the fourteenth and fifteenth centuries. It saw itself as the heir to the power of the State of Kiev. Little by little it expanded, taking advantage of the decline of the Asian invaders. Moscow, the capital, was restored and enhanced.

Bells upon Bells
Most of the buildings of the Kremlin are Byzantine in style, though some Italian influence can be seen inside. This is the case with the magnificent bell tower built by order of Ivan III at the beginning of the sixteenth century. Inside, it holds thirty-one bells. The Tsar Bell is so large that twenty people could fit inside it.

The Trans-Siberian Railroad

At the end of the nineteenth century, the Russian empire remained disconnected. The enormous distance between its western and eastern borders made it almost impossible to cross the country by land. Siberia, immense and lonely, lay between the Ural Mountains and the Pacific coast.

Communication difficulties hindered the flow of trade and the colonization of new lands, leaving much Russian territory outside the empire's effective control. There was an urgent need for a railroad that would cross the empire. It was Czar Alexander III who first took on the mighty task. In May 1891, work began on a project that, ten years later, saw the completion of 6,000 miles (9,600 kilometers) of railroad from the coast of the Baltic Sea to the empire's eastern edge at Vladivostok on the Pacific Ocean.

The work proceeded rapidly. The terrain presented no special difficulties; there were few forests to clear. Nevertheless, there were important feats of engineering, such as the bridge over the River Ob, in Novosibirsk, in central Siberia.

The train began to run in 1900.

Under ideal conditions, the trip took two weeks. But inevitably problems caused enormous delays. Sometimes there were broken tracks. In the summer Lake Baikal had to be crossed by boat; in the winter, by tracks laid over the ice. Prestigious European companies quickly launched luxury lines along the Trans-Siberian route, offering wealthy tourists the chance to travel in comfort, with sleeper coaches, gymnasiums, and piano lounges. Russian trains were much more modest, but they completed their mission. They strengthened relations between the distant parts of the empire, enhanced the well-being of its people, and helped to control and colonize Siberia.

The buildings of the citadel (the Kremlin), which had been demolished by the invaders, were rebuilt and strengthened. Then began a period of high culture.

In the sixteenth century, Ivan the Terrible awarded himself the title of Czar of All the Russias. This marked the birth of the Russian Empire.

The czars claimed infinite power, and their decrees were the only law. The czar's absolute power—both political and personal—were unquestionable realities in Russian society.

The social structure of the empire was based on the estate system. The nobility held the economic power because of the vast properties they owned. These great landowners exploited the labor of the peasants, who served under them as serfs. The serfs depended entirely upon the master. They could not leave his lands, which they worked without pay. When Russia became industrialized, some serfs even worked in factories under often inhuman conditions.

The social class in between the peasants and the nobles was rather small. It consisted of the army, the merchants, and various employees of the imperial court.

Not until the nineteenth century did a true middle class emerge, enriched by trade. The growth of this middle class helped push Russia toward industrialization, which it achieved later than the rest of Europe.

The splendors of Czarist Russia concealed an unjust social system. Here, the majority of the people lived under terribly difficult conditions. Efforts at political reform did little to improve the situation.

The Great Czars

In the eighteenth and nineteenth centuries, the czars worked to modernize the empire and to help it fit in with the rest of Europe. At the same time, they continued their conquests across the great Asiatic plain of Siberia, colonizing extensive territory. By 1700, Russia had reached the Pacific Ocean. Large-scale migrations did not begin, however, until the completion of the Trans-Siberian Railroad 200 years later.

Peter I, "the Great," greatly advanced the Europeanization process by reforming the army, the treasury, and the education system. He turned Russia into a great military power and began its industrialization.

A City of Canals
The city of St. Petersburg was built on islands in the delta of the Neva River. The city has many canals and beautiful palaces. In the upper photo is the Neo-Classical St. Isaac Cathedral.

Peter dreamed of building a great empire in the European style. To accomplish this, he abolished many centuries-old customs and traditions. He is responsible for building one of the world's most beautiful capital cities: St. Petersburg.

Catherine II continued the work of reform and made alliances with Austria and Prussia.

Under Alexander I, Russia's territory expanded and its population grew. These factors made it a leading European power. Russia acted as arbiter in the great European wars against Napoleon Bonaparte. In the mid-nineteenth century, Alexander II abolished serfdom, the unjust social system that had been handed down for centuries.

The czars' absolute power and the nation's poverty continued to stir discontent among people of many classes. First the intellectuals and people of the middle class tried to make the empire a democracy. Later, at the beginning of the twentieth century, Vladimir Lenin led the working class in a socialist revolution that gave birth to the Soviet Union.

In 1991, the Union of Soviet Socialist Republics (USSR) broke apart. The republics that formed it have declared their independence and formed a Commonwealth of Independent States, the CIS.

Historic St. Petersburg: City of Monuments

St. Petersburg is the symbol of the new Russia Peter I dreamed of: a powerful, united, European empire. It is a sharp contrast to traditional Russia, shut into itself and removed from the flow of European history.

The city was built to be the capital of the great empire. Its construction became possible after the czar seized from Sweden land along the eastern shore of the Gulf of Finland. Once again Russia had access to the Baltic Sea, after one hundred years of Swedish occupation. As soon as this territory reverted to Russia in 1702, it was fortified for protection. Immediately plans got underway for the building of an impressive city on the delta of the Neva River. It was the greatest city built in Europe in the eighteenth century and the most overwhelming demonstration of growing Russian power.

Two factors made it possible to build St. Petersburg: the availability of money and the forced labor of Russian soldiers and prisoners of war. Thus a swampy, inhospitable piece of land was transformed into a splendid city.

A Hub of Culture
St. Petersburg is laid out in a simple geometric pattern. It has three great thoroughfares. The most outstanding of these, known as the Nevskii Prospekt, runs east and west. Street artists often display their paintings along this avenue. On the right is a detail of the Smolny Convent. Above is the Hermitage. It is attached to the extraordinary Winter Palace and houses a very important collection of paintings.

The islands of the Neva River delta were joined by more than four hundred beautiful bridges. The northern forests became gardens. The countless branches at the Neva's mouth were dredged, and wharves were built for the Baltic fleet. All this was done in less than twenty years under the architect Jean Baptiste Alexandre Le Blond.

The city's layout is simple. The boulevards, squares, palaces, and public buildings possess a unique harmony. The city has three major thoroughfares. The most outstanding is the great east-west artery called the Nevskii Prospekt.

Most of St. Petersburg's architecture follows the Baroque and Neo-Classical styles. Peter I and his successors hired the most important European architects of the time to complete the monumental work that we can admire today.

The earliest buildings are Baroque in style. They are the work of two major architects. Domenico Tressini designed the Fortress of Peter and Paul, the cathedral, and the Building of the Twelve Colleges. Bartolomeo Rastrelli built the extraordinary Winter Palace, the Smolny Convent, the Church of the Resurrection, and a series of monumental palaces, including Anichkov Palace, residence of Alexander III.

The buildings constructed in the second half of the eighteenth century and during the nineteenth century are Neo-Classical. In this style the architect Jean Baptiste de la Mothe built the Academy of Fine Arts and the first Hermitage, a museum to preserve Catherine II's splendid collection of paintings.

Baroque and Neo-Classical
Baroque and Neo-Classical buildings come together in St. Petersburg with perfect harmony. In the upper photo is a detail of St. Isaac's Cathedral, built in the Neo-Classical style. Below is the Cathedral and Fortress of Peter and Paul, both Baroque. On the left are the gardens of the Summer Palace.

Constructions of Brick

The immense Red Square, the true symbol of Moscow, spreads over 805,500 square feet (74,831 square meters). At its south end is the Cathedral of St. Basil the Blessed. With its characteristic cupolas, it is one of the most beautiful monuments of Russian Orthodox art. Facing it is the city's Historical Museum. Built of red brick, it is one of the buildings that gave this great plaza its name.

Other works from this era are the Cathedral of Our Lady of Kazan by Andrei Voronykhin, St. Isaac's Cathedral by Auguste de Montferrand, and the palaces built by Rinaldi. The list goes on and on.

The historic buildings in St. Petersburg are bold and striking, showing great contrasts of style. Yet, they all combine beautifully with the natural landscape. Marble, pink granite, and golden stucco blend with the blue water of the Neva and the greenery of the parks. In addition, St. Petersburg was Russia's great cultural center.

In 1917, St. Petersburg was the city where the Bolshevik Revolution triumphed, bringing to an end the Age of the Czars.

Moscow: The Kremlin and Red Square

Kremlin is a Slavic word meaning "fortress." Many Russian cities have a kremlin, or walled section. But Moscow's Kremlin is undoubtedly the most impressive.

The earliest mention of the Kremlin's existence is in the twelfth century. Later it became prominent as the great political and religious center of the state of Moscow. The rulers lived there and erected the most extraordinary administrative and religious buildings since the founding of the Principality of Moscow. In 1328, Moscow also became the center of the Russian Orthodox Church.

The Kremlin's walled enclosure occupies 70 acres (28 hectares) and is triangular in shape. It stands on a low hill, overlooking the Moscow River.

Little remains of the original Kremlin. The oldest surviving buildings are in the southwestern section, around Cathedral Square. Most were built during the reign of Ivan III, between 1462 and 1505. In general they are Byzantine in style. But some Italian influence can be seen within, as artists and architects from Italy's Venice worked on the construction.

The cathedrals of the Annunciation, the Dormition, and the Archangel Michael all date from this era. Some of these magnificent monuments were partially connected with the Great Palace, which was built in the nineteenth century during the reign of Nicholas I.

A Seat of Politics and Religion
The first Kremlin existed in the twelfth century. In addition to being the traditional residence of the rulers, the fortress contained all of the administrative and religious buildings of the State of Moscow. Unfortunately, few buildings remain from the original Kremlin. This photo shows a view of one of the twenty-nine towers of the Kremlin wall.

Nicholas also incorporated other buildings from earlier times, such as the Church of the Virgin's Nativity. The square is crowned by the magnificent Bell Tower of Ivan III, first constructed in the sixteenth century. The tower has thirty-one bells. One of them, called the Tsar Bell, is so large that it could hold twenty people.

To the north stand the eighteenth-century Church of the Twelve Apostles and Peter the Great's arsenal (now called the Armory Palace), built in 1701.

The group is completed by the buildings that Catherine II built. Among the most outstanding is the Neo-Classical Palace of the Senate, built with a triangular floor plan. It was built between 1771 and 1785.

Outside the walled enclosure, in the eastern section, lies the immense Red Square. Covering 805,500 square feet (74,831 square meters), it is crowned to the south by the Cathedral of St. Basil the Blessed. The cathedral is one of the most beautiful monuments of Russian Orthodox art, topped with exquisite cupolas.

The Kremlin's architecture is an impressive demonstration of Russian art. The surrounding wall is topped by twenty-nine towers. They seem to watch over the Kremlin, protecting it from attack and preserving it for future generations to admire.

Petcherskaya Lavra of Kiev

Today Kiev is the capital of the republic of Ukraine. In medieval times it was the capital of the state of Rus. It was also Russia's most important religious center. There, at the end of the tenth century, the Prince of Kiev, St. Vladimir the Great, converted to Christianity and permitted the Byzantine priests to preach Christianity to the people.

The highest seat of the church's power was located in Kiev. For this reason, Kiev became the religious capital of the state. This fact has affected Kiev's history and appearance. The city has a number of important religious buildings, whose cupolas give it a distinctive skyline.

These monuments stand as a testament to Russia's past and a unique example of religious art. The first of them were built in the tenth century. Kiev is truly a "holy city." Its religious district stands on a hill, on the banks of the Dnieper River, in the southeastern section of Kiev's historic district, and is known as Petcherskaya Lavra.

Cupolas of the Holy City
In the tenth century, Vladimir the Great, Prince of Kiev, converted to Christianity. From that time on, the city became Russia's most important spiritual center. Kiev contains a cluster of important religious buildings known as the Petcherskaya Lavra. Gathered on a hill, they present an unforgettable image with their many cupolas.

The oldest building in Petcherskaya Lavra is the monastery with a maze of catacombs, known in Russian as "petcheri." There can be found countless saints' relics, which helped make Kiev famous as a sacred city. The first chronicle that mentions this district dates back to 1051. The Cathedral of the Dormition, the Church of the Trinity, and the Church of the Savior were built between the eleventh and thirteenth centuries. In addition there were many lesser buildings for the use of the worshipers, such as the refectory, of which only a few traces remain.

The Mongol invaders who overran the city partially destroyed the monuments. Some were later rebuilt, such as the Cathedral of the Dormition, which was restored in the fifteenth century.

During the seventeenth and eighteenth centuries, a new group of churches was built in the Ukrainian Baroque style. Among the best examples are the Church of All Saints and the Church of the Nativity of the Virgin, both from the seventeenth century. Other works include the bell tower and the Church of the Exaltation of the Cross, also from the eighteenth century.

Kizhi Pogost

In northern Russia, in the republic of Karelia near Lake Onega, is the region of Kizhi Pogost. Within this area is one of the most beautiful collections of medieval Russian religious architecture.

Located at the northern edge of Europe, Kizhi Pogost was introduced to Christianity during the Middle Ages by Orthodox monks.

Special Terms

Golden Horde: Mongol state that ruled Russia from the Volga region after the breakup of the large 13th-century Mongol Empire.

icon: Religious painting on a slab of wood.

Mongols: Asiatic people from the region south of Lake Baikal, unified by Genghis Khan, who conquered all of Mongolia and parts of Asia and Eastern Europe in the thirteenth century.

steppe: Bare, treeless plain.

Kiev: Religious Metropolis
Kiev was the seat of the "metropolitan," the title given to the highest Orthodox religious figure in Rus. As a result, Kiev became the state's religious capital. An example of the many religious buildings in the city is the Cathedral of St. Sophia. The upper photo shows a model of the cathedral. The lower photos show details of the interior frescoes.

The monks established religious communities in places that were easy to reach. This way, they could serve people who were scattered over a wide territory. These communities contained churches, a cemetery, and meeting halls.

Sixteenth-century chronicles already speak of Kizhi Pogost. Nevertheless, the churches that we can observe today are not the originals, which were destroyed by a fire. Instead, they were built in the eighteenth century with traditional wooden architecture, the work of anonymous Russian and Scandinavian carpenters.

The Church of the Transfiguration was the summer church. It was the largest, to accommodate the great number of worshipers who came from far-flung places. These people were completely isolated by the winter snows. Standing at the north of the group, the church is octagonal in structure and is built on several levels. It is crowned by a central cupola 120 feet (37 meters) high and by twenty-two bulb-shaped cupolas that vary in size. The cupolas are covered with aspen wood, following the tradition of Russian wooden churches. The church is divided into three separate spaces: the refectory, where the peasants gathered; the church proper, for religious ceremonies; and the altar, separated from the church by a wooden wall worked with magnificent eighteenth- and nineteenth-century icons. This separation, called the *iconostasis,* is common to all Russian Orthodox churches.

The Church of the Intercession was used in the winter and stands at the south end of the enclosure. It is smaller and simpler in structure than the summer church. It, too, is crowned with bulblike cupolas. The group is completed by a beautiful bell tower with a tentlike roof. A wooden stockade surrounds the buildings.

In their simplicity and startling majesty, the buildings are in perfect balance with the surrounding landscape.

The Historic City of Itchan Kala

South of the Amu Darya River in the heart of Asia stood the oasis of Khiva. This was the last supply point for caravans before they entered the Kara Kum Desert on their journey toward Persia.

Kizhi
Pogost

St. Petersburg

BALTIC SEA

Moscow

Kiev

ARAL
SEA

Itchan
Kala

CASPIAN
SEA

BLACK SEA

MEDITERRANEAN SEA

WORLD HERITAGE SITES

The city of Khiva, in present-day Uzbekistan, already existed in the sixth century. It was the administrative and religious center of the state of Khwarezm, a vassal state to Persia. It had become prosperous thanks to irrigation, which turned the desert into pastures and fertile fields.

Khiva had a turbulent history. It was frequently attacked, conquered, and controlled by various empires. The Arabs conquered it in 712, the Mongols took over in 1221, and in the fourteenth century the mighty Tamerlane absorbed it into his Asiatic empire. In the fifteenth century it was conquered by the Uzbekis, and in the seventeenth century it became a Russian protectorate. Since 1924 it has belonged to the republic of Uzbekistan.

During the Middle Ages, Khiva was one of Asia's great Islamic religious centers, along with Samarkand and Bukhara. Its history has left a permanent mark on its appearance and design. The city is divided into two parts. Dichan Kala, the outer city, is surrounded by a fortified wall with eleven entrance gates. Itchan Kala, the historic inner city, is surrounded by a brick wall forty feet (twelve meters) high.

The historic sector is rectangular, laid out along a north-south and an east-west axis. Its four gates stand at the north, south, east, and west ends. The great public buildings are arranged along the east-west axis. At either end stands a palace that served as the residence of the Khan of Khiva. In the northeast corner is a twelfth-century fortress converted into a luxurious palace by Alla-Kouli Khan in the nineteenth century. In the northwest stands another palace, also dating from the twelfth century. The palaces rival one another in beauty and luxury. Marble and precious woods, inlays of a thousand colors, and exquisite stuccos create a feeling of richness.

Few of the monuments built before the eighteenth century still survive. The most important of these is the tenth-century Djouma Mosque. It was restored in the eighteenth century with materials taken from other ruined buildings. Its magnificent hall has two hundred and twelve columns, creating what seems like a forest of columns. Other survivors from the original buildings are a series of houses, all with the same design: a courtyard, porticoed reception room, and private apartments.

In the twentieth century, architects kept new buildings in harmony with the original ones. They built mosques and Islamic schools such as Islam-Khod, whose minaret is the tallest in Khiva.

Remains of the Empire
The Empire of the Czars was formed at the end of the seventeenth and the beginning of the eighteenth century. It was an era of splendor for some social groups and a time of unhappiness for others. Many examples of the empire's art and architecture survive to this day, and UNESCO has designated several of them as World Heritage sites. In the photographs are the Armory Palace of Moscow's Kremlin; the Church of the Petcherskaya Lavra in Kiev; and the Winter Palace, today's Hermitage Museum, in St. Petersburg.

These Sites Are Part of the World Heritage

St. Petersburg: Historic Center and Monuments: The greatest urban creation of the eighteenth century. Baroque and Neo-Classical buildings unite in a beautiful natural setting.

Moscow: The Kremlin and Red Square: Standing on a low hill, the main buildings of the Kremlin—or fortress—date from the twelfth century. Outside the walled enclosure lies the immense Red Square.

Petcherskaya Lavra of Kiev: The "Holy City" of Kiev was begun at the end of the eleventh century.

Kizhi Pogost: This region contains one of the most beautiful and representative examples of religious architecture of medieval Russia. The churches were rebuilt in the eighteenth century in keeping with the tradition of wooden architecture.

Historic City of Itchan Kala: The city, in the heart of Asia, dates back to the sixth century and is divided into two parts: Dichan Kala, the outer city, and Itchan Kala, the inner city and historic center, surrounded by a wall forty feet (twelve meters) high.

Glossary

administration: the governing or managing of public affairs

anonymous: having an unknown name

arbiter: a middleman in a dispute

arsenal: a place for storing guns and ammunition

Baroque: an elaborately ornamented artistic style that was prevalent in the seventeenth and eighteenth centuries

catacombs: underground tombs arranged along long passageways

chronicle: a historic record of events

citadel: a fortress

cupola: a circular structure that forms a rounded ceiling or sits on top of a roof

diversity: variety; contrast

dredge: to dig into the bottom of a waterway in order to make it deeper or to remove objects

ethnic: having to do with cultural, racial, or national traits

facade: the front of a building

fragile: delicate

fresco: a piece of art in which a picture is painted into the wet plaster of a wall

industrialization: manufacturing activity

invincible: unable to be defeated

isolation: separation

medieval: having to do with the Middle Ages, a period of European history lasting from about A.D. 500 to 1500

minaret: a tall tower attached to a mosque, from which a crier calls people to prayer

navigable: able to be traveled by seagoing vessels

Neo-Classical: an artistic style that follows ancient Greek and Roman ideals

nomads: people who regularly move their residence from place to place

obscurity: state of being remote or not well known

principality: the territory of a prince

refectory: the dining hall of a monastery or school

relic: fragment of the bodily remains or of the clothing or possessions of someone (such as a saint)

splendor: brilliance, glory, or grandeur

vassal: one who is in service to a feudal lord

wharf: a dock where ships may load and unload

Index

Page numbers in boldface type indicate illustrations.

Titles in the World Heritage Series

Photo Credits

All the photographs in this volume
were taken by
Jorge de Vergara/Incafo.

Project Editor, Childrens Press: Ann Heinrichs
Original Text: Esther Carrion
Subject Consultant: Dr. James Krokar
Translator: Deborah Kent
Design: Alberto Caffaratto
Cartography: Modesto Arregui
Phototypesetting: Publishers Typesetters Inc.